WEEDS
among
SEEDS

The Art of Paying Attention

Produced with the assistance of Fluency Organization, Inc.

Graphic design: Inkwell Creative

Original cover artwork by Katarina Maksimovic.

"Potato Picker" oil on wood.

"Nobody made a greater mistake than he who did nothing because he could do only a little."—Edmund Burke

"Nobody can help everybody, but everybody can help somebody."–Denver Moore

"We are all homeless, just working our way home."

–Denver Moore

The Anderson-Vukelja Foundation is a private family foundation benefiting people in need. All proceeds from the sale of this book go to support life-changing work with the homeless.

Names used by permission in an effort to honor their identity, not to disguise it.

An Ode to an Oak Tree

A time ago in a far-away village beyond the ocean sprouted a tiny seed.

Tiny Seed struggled to grow into a tree because the village ground was hardened by rocks that could only grow weeds.

Mother Tree was wise and strong for that she could see, so she plotted a journey to the land of the fertile and green.

They uprooted their stakes and the ship set sail, the journey was long, finally they would be happy and free.

The land was lush and the hills were green and Tiny Seed sprouted into a tiny oak tree.

Mother Tree was proud and strong but couldn't contend with the plan of her Creator it would have to be.

From his breath he blew a mighty gust of wind that fell Mother Tree, for she knew it was her time to leave.

Tiny Tree's leaves shook and God told her to stay planted and take as long as she needed, for it was her time to grieve.

She did as God said and her roots grew deep and her branches grew strong for the wounded birds to nest before they flew free.

There is still plenty of room for all under the tree, and that's how she grew and became known as Dr. V.

—Teresa Butcher

Table of Contents

Chapter One

WHERE I DID NOT WANT TO BE

I hated to go there because I saw myself in them.

I didn't want to go even after I had agreed to go. I looked out my windshield at the gathering of disheveled people a few yards in front of me underneath a concrete bridge. I sat motionless in my car for several minutes, feeling as if I were staring at my own reflection in the mirror. This could happen to you, a small voice told me. This *is* happening to me, I answered.

I felt hopeless. Without purpose. The people

in front of me appeared to share much of the same aimless existence. It was very disturbing to see it–as if it were a replay of my own life.

A sudden knocking on my driver's side window broke into my thoughts. "Do you have the donuts?" a man asked, his voice muffled by the glass of my raised window.

I didn't have the donuts. I didn't even know what he was talking about. But he'd seen me, so I'd have to get out of the car now. "Are you here to volunteer?" he asked. I nodded. He hurriedly walked me over to a makeshift table and instructed me to wait there. Just then another volunteer brought over several brown boxes and stacked them on the table. He opened the lid of one of them, revealing an unappetizing jumbled mess of day old donuts with sprinkles, red jelly, and icing. I was told to put two donuts inside a baggy and stack the baggies next to me. My hands trembled as I tried prying apart the gooey concoction. I dropped some donuts because my hands were shaking so much, and I looked around to see if anyone noticed.

I was so conscious of every move I made. My eyes were twitching. My mouth was dry. I was tired. There seemed to be a lump in my throat. Several volunteers introduced themselves to me, but I couldn't remember anyone's name. They kept recognizing me, but I didn't recognize any of them.

A man whose name I later learned was Sam came to the table and quietly tucked a baggy of donuts inside his well-worn jacket. He smiled his gratitude in a broad mouthful of rotten teeth. I visibly cringed, but he didn't seem to notice and shuffled off to lean against one of several grey columns holding up the bridge and consumed his breakfast. That's the next step for *you*, I told myself. I had also stopped caring about my own appearance. I just didn't have the energy to take good care of myself. Even brushing my teeth was an effort. I saw my future like a terrible vision I didn't want but could not avoid. Everything I observed that morning I translated into a direct connection between my future and their present existence.

I had people who loved me and I was a doctor, for goodness' sake. Realistically, I would never be homeless. But I didn't see it that way then. I couldn't see it. Besides, they once had people who loved them, too. Where were those people now? The men and women I encountered that morning were so disturbed and their interpretation of their environment so disconnected. But my own assessment of what was going on around me was also off. Looking back, I can see why people commit suicide. I really can. Because you don't see the world the way it really is. It's distorted. You feel that people don't want you, and because of that, you become even more isolated until you just bottom out.

At the height of my issues, I didn't want to go out anywhere because I was convinced that people didn't want to be around me. I was no fun. So I further isolated myself. Meeting friends to watch TV programs that I'd enjoyed for years was such a stretch. I forced myself to do it because I felt that I just had to do something. My patients thought they could help me. They sent cards, presents, cookies, soup, and homemade banana bread because they knew something was wrong. And yet I dismissed their concern as misdirected effort and gave it all away. I solemnly picked up their expression of love in the form of chocolate chip cookies or whatever, walked over to the patients' lounge, and left it there. I could not connect to the people who were reaching out to me. Everyone seemed so far away. I felt entirely alone, even though I was surrounded by so many.

For the first time in my practice, when a patient's test results were not favorable, I responded as if those results were my own. As if it were all happening to me. I felt devastated to the point where a terminal patient one day was consoling me! "It's going to be okay, Dr. V," he said, his brow furrowed with concern.

"You did everything you can. It's going to be okay." It was a strange reversal of roles where I felt all their pain and all their suffering. Ten times worse. But I was always the strong one before. I had always challenged everyone to "Live, live. Do not just exist." I was not living. I was barely existing. People had often told me that they enjoyed my memoir, a book I wrote years prior about my journey from Yugoslavia to America. One day I picked up a copy from my bookshelf and tried to re-read it, but I didn't recognize myself. The person who wrote this was optimistic and invincible. I said to myself, Who is this? I did not know anymore.

"You just have to pray," my friend said to me confidently one day.

"I am praying!" I answered quickly, but I wasn't getting anywhere in my prayers. My pastor says to P.U.S.H. when you go through a hard time—**P**ray **U**ntil **S**omething **H**appens. I'd been praying and nothing had been happening. If only it were that easy. If pushing was the sole answer to my problems, I would have had the biggest biceps in the world. I was pushing all day long. Seriously. I was pushing and pushing and pushing.

I would make multiple visits daily to the pharmacist in our clinic. He was my sounding board, and I always asked the same questions. When will I feel better? Am I going to be better? He told me that I was in a dark, deep valley. "And one day you will climb to the top of the mountain again and be free," he assured me. But at the moment all I thought about was that God would never come through for me. There were times when I would go to bed at the end of the day and think, Why can't I die in my sleep? Recently several people my age group had died in their sleep, but not me! I felt jealous! That would be so easy. I would put on nice pajamas each night so that in case my husband had to call 911 at least I would look good when they brought me to the ER where I knew everyone. But no, I would wake up every morning and drag myself out of bed to face the day all over again. Even God did not want me!

I became distressed when another friend, who

was also trying to help me, asked, "Are you grateful?" "Of course I'm grateful," I had said. "Why wouldn't I be grateful? I have everything." But I was saying that because it sounded good. It was the appropriate thing to say, but I didn't feel it. There was no feeling behind a lot of things that I was saying. I felt empty. It was like I was on medication, but I was not even taking anything! I couldn't cry. I couldn't feel. I was lost. I was empty.

Practicing medicine had been my life and identity, and it had all changed. For one thing, there was much less patient contact. The advent of electronic record keeping created so much more distance separating us. The computer became a wall between us and the patients—a bridge so difficult for me to cross. I spent a lot of time on documentation, which made me feel even more removed from my patients. Their journey of care was fragmented. I was no longer the only one helping them from the starting point to the finish line. Many other care providers and physicians were now wedged between us. There was still a positive connection, but it wasn't the same. Before, I knew everything that was happening to my patients, down to every mouth sore and even their ingrown toenails. But now with the change in medicine, a team of doctors took care of my patients when they were admitted to the hospital. I was no longer my patients' "lifeline," and I often wouldn't even know that they were hospitalized.

I now know that I was experiencing "moral injury." When someone or something transgresses someone's deeply held beliefs and expectations about the fundamental way life should be, it's a moral injury. It is much more painful than burnout. I was not burned out—burn out means you cannot work anymore. I could work. I worked all the time. I loved my work. I was just grieving my inability to care for my patients in the way I felt they should be cared for—the way I'd always cared for them throughout my medical practice. I was desperately trying to change a system that was not going to change and it hit me hard. Harder than anything I'd experienced in my life to that point. And I had experienced a lot. I'd been homeless in Europe throughout my childhood because my mother was so outspoken against communism and we had to keep moving. I had spent a week being interrogated with her in prison when I was a young teen. We'd lived in a refugee camp under the threat of being deported. My mother and I had finally escaped and arrived in America. But this new state of medicine towered over me like an immovable mountain. It was not going to change. I had to change. But I didn't know how.

Mrs. Goodman was a small lady with stage IV breast cancer. At the end of every medical appointment after she reviewed all of her concerns, she would lean over toward me with a smile on her face and ask in a very soft voice, "And how is my doctor?" She genuinely cared about me as a person.

I would generally make something up that I felt I could say to her that would satisfy her and keep me from having to bare my soul. Finally one day I felt as if I might cry when she asked me that question, but the strange thing was that I couldn't shed a single tear. My body was empty of everything—even tears. I squeezed my eyes, but nothing happened. Without a word, Mrs. Goodman got up from the examining table and stood in front of me. She put her arms around me and to my surprise started rocking me back and forth very slowly like you would a baby.

I went absolutely limp in her arms and we stood there in silence for several minutes. "Don't let him have you," she finally said softly. "He wants you."

"Who wants me?" I asked.

"The devil," she replied matter-of-factly.

I thought, Oh my gosh…she is one of those people who talks about devils. I pushed away from her embrace slightly and jokingly made horns with my fingers above my head. "You mean, the devil?"

She smiled. "You're making fun of it. That's okay. You can call him whatever you want… Satan, negative energy, bad influence. But whatever you call it, he wants you."

I relaxed a little in her arms once more as she continued.

"How do you think he's going to get you? He's going to make you hate your gift. Your partners in this practice are great physicians, but you have a gift. You have a gift, and he wants you to hate it." That very morning I'd already said under my breath a thousand times how much I despised computers. I had to make twelve clicks with the mouse before I could get to the information I needed about a patient.

"You're angry about something you can't change," she explained, her words falling softly on my ear. "So why don't you look at that computer and think to yourself how this could be helpful?"

This little lady was talking to me as if I were a child. But something in me was curious about what she might say next. I asked weakly, "What do you mean?"

She was on a roll now. "Well, do you think this hospital is going to get rid of all the computers because Dr. Vukelja doesn't like them?"

I said nothing. Was this a joke?

"Well, *do* you?" she wanted to know.

Eyes wide, I shook my head "no."

Satisfied with my answer, Mrs. Goodman continued, "That's right. They're not going to change. *You* have to change, and then everything else will change."

And you know what? Something clicked. I drove home that night, woke up the next day, and felt pretty good for the first time for a few hours. I thought, Oh it's just today. I was sure it was going to pass. But the next day I felt good for most of the day, and then the next day I was okay all day. I thought to myself, My gosh maybe it's happening. All the PUSHing might finally be paying off. But it was too early to tell for certain.

Chapter Two

TWO STEPS FORWARD ONE STEP BACK

When I first encountered Church Under the Bridge, I was shopping in the bakery section of Sam's Club discount store one Saturday morning. I noticed a man who was buying several big boxes full of donuts. I pointed to the treats and said, "You must have a really big family to eat all those." He told me they were not for him. "I'm taking them to Church Under the Bridge," he said.

"What's that?" I asked, trying to picture some sort of church building underneath one of the few bridges we had in my small community. He explained how a group of volunteers provided breakfast and a church service for the homeless every Saturday morning. I remember briefly thinking that I would like to do that one day, but then I forgot about it. It was several years later when a patient invited me to go with her to Church Under the Bridge one morning. The timing could not have been worse for me to try to reach out to help others. She had no idea how much I was struggling at the time, but I did not think I could tell her no.

It was a Friday when she invited me, and I knew that I was staring down the barrel of two days off when I would have nothing to do. I was planning to spend most of it the way I had been spending all of my days off lately: lying in bed, hyper-focusing on how much things had changed at work and pondering all the reasons why I could not handle that change. At least I was busy at work, but on the weekends, I found that I wasn't interested in doing anything. There are just so many hours you can walk your dogs. I was completely focused on my symptoms and my needs and my total preoccupation with wondering if I'd ever be the same again. I was mourning my past, my health, and the way things used to be. I spent hours swiping through pictures on my phone, looking at the past. I remember this was fun, I'd say to myself. Oh, I remember that, that was great. But I wasn't living in the present. I was living in this vague nowhere land where there was no sense of time.

I decided that I did not really want to spend another Saturday doing that, so that Friday evening after dinner I casually told my husband, "I'm going to go to Church Under the Bridge tomorrow." Knowing how down I'd been, he thought that was a great idea. But Saturday morning, I could not get out of bed. It was just hard. Finally I got up and got dressed, but then I changed my mind and told him, "I'm just going to stay here."

He cocked an eyebrow at me over the book he was reading. I started to waver. At least if I went, I would have something to do. And that would get me out of my world temporarily. At the clinic with my patients I was fine, but it was impossible for me at the time to make decisions about my own personal life, large or small. Finally, I forced myself to get in the car and headed downtown to the bridge.

That first morning at Church Under the Bridge was so cold and rainy. As I took my station at the donut table, I was surprised to see there were children in line. They looked so cold and their feet were wet, and I knew exactly how that felt. I suddenly remembered being in freezing temperatures in Yugoslavia with my mother as a child as we patiently waited outside the Seventh Day Adventist Church for some strangers to volunteer to take us home with them. It was well known that if you stood in front of that church, someone would eventually take you in for the night and provide you with at least a decent meal and a warm bed. My shoes were blue suede with white trim and the thinnest soles you can imagine. In a communist country, you take what you can get. As I shifted my weight between my icy feet wondering which strangers would take us home, I began daydreaming of a time when I would never again have wet feet.

When I came to the United States, that was one of the key components of the American dream: having warm and dry feet. Later as an adult, I bought my first pair of waterproof boots and went outside the store to test them in a puddle. Before the clerk could argue, "Hey, you can't do that!" I jumped right in the water. My feet remained dry! I came back inside and announced proudly, "I'll take them."

So when I peeled another glazed donut from the underside of a chocolate glazed, I thought about how glad those kids would be just to have warm shoes. After the volunteers distributed all the donuts, we all sat together under the bridge. Some people sang worship songs and a man preached a sermon. I could imagine that the people were still hungry, and we were so cold, and yet many seemed warm sitting there together worshipping. I was just so surprised by their contentment. Afterward, I stood around desperately waiting for the event to be over and noticed how many of the homeless men and women had tics. I breathed in the smell of urine and stale body odor with every breath. Many of them were talking to each other about things I could not understand, as if they spoke a foreign language. I just couldn't follow their conversation at all. They were smoking and once in a while someone would laugh, grey smoke rising from their breath and their leathery face contorting in a scene straight from a horror movie.

People told me the homeless always ask you for money. That day a woman did ask me for money. I told her that I'd buy some of the beautiful popsicle stick crosses she'd made and brought with her, all bejeweled with paint and ribbon. I was standing beside her admiring her work when I saw John, a tall black man at six-foot-five dressed all in white and wearing a blue hat with Chicago embroidered on it. He was like God himself posted there, so clean in contrast to the rest with only a few specks of dark paint on his shirt. He stood still, almost like a statue, before he looked me straight in the eye and started walking toward me. He picked up one of the crosses and looked at it.

Taken aback by his bold presence, I asked, "Do you come here often?" I really didn't know how else to strike up a conversation.

He smiled and responded in a rich, velvety voice, "I come here for a gratitude check." As I listened, he began talking about his story. He was once homeless, and now he had so much to be grateful for.

I was stunned by what I heard. I had kept saying for months how grateful I was and never felt anything close to the depth of gratitude John obviously felt.

"Excuse me," I said to him, reaching in my pocket and grabbing my iPhone. "Can I record you?" He smiled, not sure how to interpret my request. "No, really," I assured him, "I need to hear this every morning. And several times a day." He looked at me puzzled, but he agreed to let me record him. Now, the second time around was not as good as the first time, but what he had to say was still pretty good.

When I felt sure that I had stayed long enough to satisfy my patient who had invited me, I got in my car to leave, but I did not go home right away. I did not even start the car, despite it being twenty-five degrees outside. I was mesmerized by all the homeless huddled together. They had each other. But I felt so alone. I could hardly bear the secret I carried of becoming one of them someday. I wondered if things would get so bad that one day I would be the one picking up trash in the street, searching for something I could use because I no longer had anything. What if I became homeless again?

I left my volunteer post there exhausted and certain of one thing. I would never return there again. Never! I finally came back home and I told my husband, "This was the worst experience ever. I'm never going to go back." I couldn't believe that at the beginning of my medical career I wanted to be like Mother Teresa. I loved her work among the poor. I even chose a rotation in Kenya to live among patients in a leprosarium in Busia when I was a medical resident. Back then I envisioned myself going into the streets, wanting to care for and do the best I could for those whom no one cares for. And now I was repulsed by what I saw under the bridge. I was frightened. I was no longer able to help them; I was on the other side needing help just like they did.

One day soon after I saw John's recording on my phone. I hesitantly pushed "play," and as his supple voice talked to me about being grateful, for a brief moment it seemed possible that maybe the light might finally shine again. As time went on, I realized I could not get the homeless people out of my mind. Even though I was working at the clinic and reaching out to people every day, I felt that I had to return to the place that was so frightening to me. To a place that I wanted to like, but was repulsive to me. The feeling haunted me for months and I knew I would have no peace until I returned.

When I arrived under the bridge for the second time, it was as if no time had passed at all. There was the same stack of boxes full of donuts and many of the same people milling about. Same toothless smiles, same tics and twitches, and the same need for those warm shoes. I braced myself for what looked like another rainy day, but then the blue sky began to appear and the rain went away. It was strange. As the sun peeked out between the clouds, I felt different. I walked around after my donut shift was over and tried overhearing some conversations.

I slowly realized these people are not "weirdos." They have stories, they built a past, they share emotions, they have or had families at one time. One of the volunteers noticed that I must have looked a little lost and pointed to a young man wearing a red shirt sitting by himself in a chair. "Go and talk to him," she suggested. "Ask to hear his story. You'll be amazed."

I walked over and introduced myself. I asked to hear how he came to be homeless, and I was in no way prepared for what I heard. He and his pregnant wife had been walking on a sidewalk when a man driving a car on that same street had a seizure and ran the vehicle up on the sidewalk. His wife and their baby were killed. He smiled when he told me the name of his unborn baby and I asked, "How do you live through pain like that?"

He said, "You know, it's God. I know they are in heaven and someday I will see them again." This little fragment of his story stayed with me. It's all I have of any of the homeless people I've met there since—tiny remnants of this memory and that, never a whole picture of their life story. I can only retell the pieces of what they let me know about them.

"Hey Doc—where have you been?" someone asked, interrupting our conversation. I'm known as

Dr. V in town because most people cannot say my last name. "V" is for Victory, I used to say. It was fitting for an oncologist. But I was far from feeling victorious then. I was more comfortable going by what they called me under the bridge: Dr. D (Doctor Donuts). For a moment I thought about calling myself Banana Girl because we handed those out too, but I felt that title should go to someone younger.

I turned and saw Curly, a homeless man who was making bracelets the last time I was there. I thought he was going to want me to buy more bracelets. But he didn't. He just wanted to say hello and welcome me back. Others started to say hello. "We haven't seen you. Where have you been?" "You been doing okay, Doc?"

I went home that day more confused than I'd ever been. *They* were glad to see *me*. They noticed me. And then I felt guilty because I didn't notice them. I didn't see them. I was just there stuffing donuts into bags and handing out bananas in order to have a few moments of peace when I didn't have to worry about my own turmoil. Was I even there for the right reason? I couldn't say. But I had a feeling that I would be back the next week to find out.

The next Saturday it was no easier to get out of bed. I eventually got in my Mercedes wagon and made my way downtown. I put my plastic gloves on and dipped my hands again into the box of gooey donuts and started separating them. But then something interesting happened. I looked up to greet a man and handed him a pair of glazed donuts. He just stared at the baggy and said, "I don't want those. I want that one." And he pointed to something that had once been a sugar cake donut but was now an unrecognizable squished piece of dough with mixed icing all over it.

I joked with him that it didn't look like a cake donut anymore but he said, "I *know* it's a cake donut." I handed it to him and he went away satisfied. The man after him requested a blueberry donut. It was interesting because I thought we only had chocolate and glazed. But then I looked closer in the box and he was right. There were a few blueberry donuts in there. They knew their stuff. Over time I would learn that each man and woman had a special order. Someone would come up and I would remember they like sprinkles. It's just like when you go to your favorite restaurant and say, "I'll have the usual." My knowing that little detail about what kind of donut they liked would make them feel so connected and cared for.

Within a few weeks I took on the responsibility of buying the donuts on Saturdays because I knew which ones everyone wanted. I would need to get the blueberry ones. I had to get the sprinkle ones. When I pulled up under the bridge, I honked my horn and several of the homeless men hustled over to help me carry the boxes.

After about a month of serving on Saturday mornings, I found I couldn't sleep one night. I got up from my bed and wandered from one room to the next, watching some mindless television or reading. I was so tired, but I could not drift off. I thought about

Mrs. Goodman telling me that I had a gift. But my next thought was about all that was chipping away at that gift, the gift that God had given me. I was irate at some of the medical expenses of my patients over what I considered to be the most trivial things. Nothing was free anymore. All of it was taking away from my gift little by little until I feared nothing useful would be left. I'm a survivor by nature. Anyone who escapes communism and flees to another country is a survivor. And now I was just dying slowly.

My partners misinterpreted what was happening to me as "typical burnout" and suggested I start taking an extra day off. So now I had Mondays and Tuesdays off, which meant four days in a row to lay in bed or walk my dogs. Most people would be excited to have a long weekend every week. Not me. And certainly not my dogs. My dogs would be walking for four or five hours around the brick streets in my neighborhood or on the treadmill next to mine as I walked and watched some recorded television shows that used to be my favorites. Before, I had so much to do but never enough time. Now I had so much free time—but I felt I had nothing meaningful to do with it.

One day I was walking my dogs in the park around the corner from my house and they got away from me. I tried to scream their names but nothing came out. My vocal cords were frozen. I had no voice. It was as if it were too much effort for my body to summon the energy to scream. I felt the end was near.

After a while the dogs returned on their own and I started to walk them down another street. But then my Dalmatian stopped and looked up at me with eyes that asked, "Can't I go home now?" I wanted to go home too. But I didn't want to face the emptiness waiting for me when I walked back through the front door.

Chapter Three
RETURNING TO MY PAST

My mother gave me lots of advice, but one thing she always told me when I was growing up was to side with the weak ones and protect them. I didn't always understand her wisdom because there were times when we were the ones who needed protecting. My father and mother had been put in exile for their outspoken anti-communism views. A sworn enemy of the state, my mother was sometimes more afraid of our own family members with close ties to the Communist Party than we were of going home with strangers.

But when I grew older I understood why she stood in the gap for people whom society considered less than desirable. My mother grew up in a wealthy family in Yugoslavia but Sida, her mother, did not see her oldest daughter, Katarina, as a valuable commodity. Sida made it obvious that she favored her younger daughter, Koka and spoiled her at every opportunity. She even sent Katarina to live at a French convent for a year as a young girl when Sida was unable to care for both children after a shocking family crisis. Sida's husband, a well-respected judge named Boris, was brutally murdered one day after the brothers of a convicted criminal attacked and killed him for revenge.

Sida criticized Katarina constantly throughout her life, drawing unfavorable comparisons between the two sisters and telling my mother she would never amount to anything. As a teen, tensions mounted between her and her mother and Mama was sent away once more to live with her grandfather Svetislav who lived three hundred miles away. She spent the greater part of a year there and several summers as well. My mother clung to her grandfather because he adored her. She was his little girl until the day he died, and my mom named me Svetislava after him.

When the girls became young adults, their mother enrolled them in an elite all-girls business school. Although Katarina could not compete with her sister's beauty and refined elegance, she far surpassed her in intellect. Mama excelled at business school and her sister struggled to keep up. It was the early 1940s and many of their classmates at the school were Jewish. Mama became best friends with several Jewish girls who told her stories about friends and relatives who were being taken away from their homes by Germans in the dead of night.

Mother listened intently to them as they whispered rumors about camps filled with Jewish people. They took away whole families, separating the men from the women and children, and no one ever heard from them again. One day several German authorities gathered in the school's lobby unannounced. Mama and her friends saw a few of their friends being taken away and loaded into waiting vans. Mama ran downstairs from her room to find out what was going on and looked up in time to see one of her friends who lived next door to her suddenly jump out a window to her death. The poor girl was convinced the Nazis were coming for her next because she had a hunchback. She was certain that she would be eliminated because of her imperfection. After my mother witnessed her friend's suicide, she became consumed with the desire to protect those who could not protect themselves.

My mother appeared very Jewish herself and favored her father, Boris. She had a plain face with curly brownish hair, a protruding nose with a large bump, hazel eyes, olive complexion, and freckles. She was often stopped on the street and interrogated by German officials who wanted to know why she wasn't wearing the yellow star patch on her clothing, as was required for all Jews. Mama did not find this offensive and was proud in a way to identify with people who were familiar with persecution.

The Jews were seen by many as undesirable weeds: unfit for use and more trouble than they were worth. They believed that the Jewish race needed to be extracted and extinguished, like weeds in a garden. And they were doing it with chemical poison, just like weeds. In Yugoslavia, the communists clearly favored Gamal Nasser, the president of Egypt. But my mother was a vocal supporter of Israel. She saw the beauty in the Jewish people and admired their tough resolve.

My friend Edie Eger is a Nazi war camp survivor and spent her life after the war speaking to groups about the atrocities she experienced. She told me how she felt that the prison guards were the real prisoners because she was able to escape through her vivid imagination about a life of freedom—a life that she might never see. My mother had a similar optimistic gene and did much the same thing as a child. Mama rebelled against the way she was treated at home and dreamed of escaping to another life. She didn't have the glamorous lifestyle that her mother gave to her sister, but Katrina carried a secret. She knew that one day she would be free.

After the end of World War II, the political climate in Yugoslavia began to change. Josip Broz Tito led the country into a distinctive brand of communism that became known as Titoism. Although independent of the formal Communist Party of Russia, it carried the same repressive flavor. The new regime snuffed out any flicker of perceived reluctance to join the party ranks.

In a country that was becoming less and less free in terms of personal expression, my mother grew more and more outspoken. Despite the risks, she could not keep from sharing her political viewpoints with anyone who would listen. A young revolutionary, she went to prison three times, serving one-year sentences each time. During her imprisonment, they let her out into the sunlight once a day. She believed that they would have put her away for longer periods, but since the prosecutor was the brother of a friend, she was shown leniency. On several occasions, Katarina attempted to escape Yugoslavia. Once she tried to get through Bulgaria—the closest border visible from the city limits. However they caught her each time and returned her to prison. This record of her escape attempts would haunt my mother long after I was born, when we were much more desperate to get out, and make it that much more difficult for us to leave.

Mama dreamed big. She had a lifelong wish to move to another country. After I was born and spent my childhood moving place to place with Mama, we eventually escaped to a refugee camp in Austria.

"We want to denounce our citizenship," Mama had announced to the guard outside the Austrian camp in perfect German, one of several languages she spoke fluently. She promptly handed over the Yugoslav passports we had waited eleven years to receive. It was a bold move on my mother's part, but it was understood that Austria had to accept you into their country if you denounced your citizenship by

47

surrendering your passport.

That moment marked the day Mama and I lost our Yugoslavian citizenship, which I have never regained to this day. In the refugee camp she zeroed in on Australia as her next home. It must have been the propaganda films from other countries that they made the refugees watch to help them determine where they wanted to immigrate. I think she was drawn to it because there was so much land available for such a small population. She read a lot throughout her life and lived vicariously through a lot of the books and characters because she didn't have anything exciting in her own life. But her vision of the future was so clear in her mind that when I was old enough to realize that we were homeless and not only that but also stateless, I just rested in her vision of a better life. I went along with it because she promised me, she *promised* me, that it was all going to be okay.

We spent a year in the refugee camp awaiting the opportunity to immigrate to another country where we could be free. But the opportunity never came and we awoke one day to discover we would be sent back that morning to Yugoslavia. As we boarded the deportation bus, we knew Tito's regime would not welcome anyone who had escaped their borders, and we were sent directly to prison for authorities to question us. We remained there one week.

When we walked out of the prison doors, we were strangers in a city where we knew no one. Absolutely no one. My mother dropped me off at the home of a woman whose boyfriend we'd just met on the deportation bus. The woman felt threatened by Mama for some reason and would only allow me to stay if my mother found another place to stay.

Mama had nowhere else to go, so she kissed me goodbye and left. This was the darkest night of her life. She followed the railroad tracks to a church and decided to go inside to say her final prayers before committing suicide by throwing her body in front of a passing train. She settled into one of the carved wooden pews at the back. A cleaning lady was busy polishing one of the railings near the front and did not notice my mother come in.

"What kind of church is this?" my mother asked quietly, her voice echoing through the empty chamber.

When she learned it was a Catholic church, she frowned. "Can I talk with a priest?" she asked. Without a word, the cleaning woman left her post and went through a doorway to the left to find the priest.

My mother planned to tell him how upset she was with the Catholics. A lifetime ago when she was eighteen, Mama had married an Italian soldier named Nino Cardarullo on a whim after the bombing of Belgrade during the spring of 1941. He was injured and hospitalized soon after where they amputated both legs. Without warning one day his unit moved him. She tried for years to find her new husband but never could. Marrying Nino in a Catholic ceremony rendered her later attempts to annul the marriage useless. Her letters to the Vatican went unanswered. Mama didn't know whether her husband was alive, missing or dead, but she could not get divorced. This complicated our emigration options because we were stuck in Yugoslavia until she could prove she was no longer married.

So when the Jesuit priest named Father Cobi came in that dark night when she was so close to giving up, she wanted to let him have it. This was all the Church's fault! As she spoke to Father Cobi, she clutched a well-worn plastic bag that contained all our legal documents. Her birth certificate (as well as mine), her certificate of marriage to Nino, and other legal documents were all crammed into this bag that she never let out of her sight.

Mama began explaining her entire story. How

she had lived with her mother and sister in Belgrade and had married an Italian in a Catholic church. How she was a political refugee and had met my father in exile and given birth to me. How we had traveled as far as Austria but couldn't stay because we didn't meet the immigration criteria of any other countries. And now she had just gotten out of prison and had left her daughter with a stranger.

All the while, Father Cobi never said a word. When she was through explaining, he asked to see her wedding certificate. She dug through the bag until she found the document and carefully unfolded it to show the priest. He never looked at Mama, only the paper.

"It's my signature at the bottom of this certificate," he said.

He looked up at Mama and then they both broke out into small smiles. Twenty years ago, in a church halfway across the country, Father Cobi had been the priest who married two young lovers, Katarina and Nino Cardarullo.

That night we became two of three women allowed to live among the brothers. Mama came back and got me and Father Cobi took us to a woman on their compound who housed missionaries. She offered us a room in her small apartment. The modestly furnished place was on the third floor and overlooked the church. She served us bowls of hot soup, and I swore I had never tasted anything so good.

"I'm sorry there is only one bed," the woman apologized after she showed us to our room. She turned down the covers and snapped on the lamp on the bedside table. Mama and I shared a bed until I was an adult. We slept with our heads and feet at opposite ends so we could both fit. The small, metal-framed bed with clean sheets and soft blanket tucked in around the edges was better than our former prison cell with its wooden bench intentionally placed on an incline to prevent rest.

I think that is when Mama began to believe that there was a larger picture forming. There were no accidents. No coincidences. The story of her faith and how she found it would highly influence my own journey.

Chapter Four

IN SEARCH OF A GENUINE FAITH

Mama was not religious then. Up until that time, Mama had identified herself as Greek Orthodox because her aristocratic family was a member of the Greek Orthodox church, although only as a formality. Living among the Jesuit community she saw things very differently. She realized that there was something or someone like God arranging our journey. The Jesuits worked tirelessly, and we also worked all day painting window frames and doors just so we could eat one meal at night and watch religious films projected on a white sheet hung on a wall.

She also saw that the Jesuits practiced their faith in a simple and genuine manner, something she'd never seen in the Greek Orthodox church where everything was so elaborate. The brothers had two shirts—one on their backs and one in the wash. They had taken a vow of poverty; they were good people. In a country where religion is not very respected, they took their faith seriously and gave to others as they had need. Everything they had, they gave to people who could use it. They were her type of people and she admired their sincere love for their fellow man.

I was also impressed with the Jesuits and how they cared for others. I had always been the new kid on the block during my childhood, changing schools constantly. I was tall and mature looking and looked more like the teacher than a student in the few school pictures I have. I just didn't fit anywhere. My mom didn't fit either. She wasn't making cookies for our classroom or helping me with my homework.

She was usually somewhere reading a book. When we did have the funds to rent a little room of our own, I remember often making eggs for dinner while Mama finished the last chapter of her favorite book. We were a different family. We didn't have a father at home. He was in another city under house arrest and I only saw him for a few minutes once in my entire life. Nothing about us was like anyone else I knew.

I learned from the Jesuits about Father Damien, a priest who dedicated his life to the care of lepers on Molokai off the coast of the Big Island in Hawaii. That's when I decided I wanted to help those who were different. The ones who were all alone; the ones nobody wanted. I could protect the weak ones as my life's calling.

I became very religious during our time with the Jesuits and quickly outpaced my mother in devotion. She spent a lot of time praying and writing down all the things she was praying for. But I wanted to be in the church. I would kneel on the cobblestones inside the chapel for hours until my knees throbbed.

I felt that suffering was part of my training so I could understand the needs of those who suffer. That idea was very attractive to me because then I could say I was one of them. I would no longer be the outsider. I would not care for them because I pitied them. I would care because I understand pain.

My mom remained Greek Orthodox throughout her life, but I was nothing when I was young. I had never been baptized but our Jesuit mentor, Father Svoljshak, recommended that I find a couple who could support my spiritual upbringing. A couple named the Schmidts stepped up and they became my rich godparents, except they were not very giving. I was baptized and my newly minted godparents gave me a little chain with a cross, anchor, and a heart with the words Hope, Love, Faith. That was the only thing I ever received from my benefactors.

But my mother dove in headfirst. She suddenly wanted to become Catholic too and got baptized. She began learning about Mother Teresa and the devotion to the Sacred Heart and fell in love with

Catholic imagery and Catholic art. She became the Jesuits' housekeeper and cleaned all the sculptures in the church every week, slowly taking in every detail as she flossed between each toe and every fold in their robes. She took so much pleasure in that job. When you're in a church service, you're several feet away from these sculptures behind the wooden pews. No one got close to these beautiful Italian works of art. Only my mother.

She never talked about the big picture, but she always said there is something called destiny. There was a plan, and we had to go through all that we'd been through, she told me. She never asked, "Why does this happen to us?" She said it *has* to be this way. To her, we were never stuck in a situation. She never said, "My gosh, I can't believe we are back on the street!"

Life to her was more like an agility trial that you see the dogs do on television—running up and down ramps, through plastic tubes, and weaving through flags on the course. She always knew there was more ahead. There was something about her that did not see reality as most people did. At times she would say, "I'm a well-informed optimist." She could be critical, but she never wanted to call herself a pessimist. Most of the time, nothing could not knock her down. She was indestructible and almost not human. She didn't see how bleak the darkness, only how bright the stars.

My mother and I never owned Bibles. Someone gave me a book when I was baptized that was about all the saints, and Mama received a Mormon Bible when we were living in New York in the Seventies. She took notice one day of two young men wearing black suits and white shirts riding bicycles. Their straight-laced appearance was such a contrast with all the craziness that was New York at the time—chanting Hare Krishnas and long-haired men and women (no bra) with bell-bottom pants and big platform shoes.

True to her nature, my mom flagged the boys down and asked them what they were doing. That's when we learned that they were Mormon missionaries and would be staying in New York for two years. "I bet you miss your mom and dad," she said and they nodded. "I tell you what," she continued, "come over to our house for dinner on Wednesday and I will make you a homecooked meal." She gave them our address.

They started coming to our home for dinner every week. My mother would tell them stories, and they would share pictures of their family with us. They loved my mother. One night she told them she might want to become Mormon. They had told her about all the stores of food the Mormon Church had stowed away for the end of the world. My mom could appreciate the idea of being prepared for a rainy day. We had never been in a position to anticipate and stay ahead of our needs. We just had to go with the flow. Being a step ahead was appealing. But in the end she didn't become a Mormon because they did not have patron saints like they did in the Catholic church.

"I would be a Mormon in a second if you only had

St. Jude," she assured them, referring to the patron saint of lost causes. Several of my professors at the Uniformed Services University of Health Sciences in Maryland where I would receive my medical training were Mormons. I went to the beautiful Washington D.C. Mormon Temple to study many afternoons. It reminded me of the Magic Kingdom castle in Disneyworld. But I remained loyal to the Catholic church since they sponsored me to come to the United States. I thought I would never change until I moved to Tyler and became a member of a Baptist church where I am today. But it was a struggle because I initially felt as though I was being disloyal.

When I attended a Jesuit nursing school in Belgium, I would spend hours in the Catholic church, during and after mass, just meditating and praying. When the priest served communion, I went forward to receive it. I cupped my hands and was told that I was a sinner so I could not touch the bread. Instead, I had to open my mouth and let the priest drop in the piece of bread because they believed it really was the body of Christ himself. It wasn't just a piece of dry bread and a little grape juice. It was an entirely different way of seeing something. I got the message that I was a sinner—but it would be years before I would discover there was much more to the story.

The Catholic services I attended were all in Latin. I didn't know half of what they were saying, so the words became a soothing mantra. It was almost like meditation, saying the same Hail Mary over and over again. It was just so comforting.

By the time my mom had lived in America many years, she was far ahead of me spiritually speaking. My mom also went through a period when she became very melancholic. We had lived in America several years, but she was missing her country. She painted voraciously and most of her paintings were scenes in Yugoslavia. We were not farmers, but I have many paintings of hers depicting cows, sheep, and land. She connected with all these elements of nature that she missed about her home in order to comfort herself.

When I was thirty-four years old, I finally moved out of the flat I shared with my mother in D.C. to live on my own—something I had never done before. I was now a practicing physician. I wanted to try my wings. My independence did not go over well with her, to put it lightly, and she prayed desperately, asking God for a miracle to get me back.

She wasn't afraid of dying. She was afraid of leaving me and feared being left alone. But death? No. My mother never talked about it. Life was about conquering. It wasn't about losing. It was moving on to the next thing and the next. And then one day when she was sixty-two and I was thousands of miles away in Alaska on my first vacation with some friends, she moved on to the next and final thing: heaven.

I told the homeless men and women in my community my story one day as part of the worship service. I said that I was "one of them" and they laughed at first. "I know you think, 'Here is this rich doctor driving a Mercedes, and she lives in this big house, and she is married to a doctor.' I know what you guys think. But you have no idea where I come from. The only way I could be *here* is because I've been *there*."

Chapter Five

ROOTS AND WEEDS

The reason why I'm connecting more to my mom is because I'm now just a few years older than she was when she died. My mother was more than my mom—she was a driving force throughout my life. And it's surprising to me to find how much like her I have become.

When I felt lost and was trying to reconnect with my purpose in life, I thought a lot about my mother. I found comfort in doing some of the same things she used to do. I began praying very specifically for people who asked me to pray for them and for some who didn't ask. When people asked my mom to pray for her, she did. She never said, "I'll pray for you" and then forgot about it. She meant it. In my clinic I usually don't ask patients if I can pray for them. I just pray for them. Some people say, "Oh, I don't pray" to which I say, "You don't have to pray, I'm going to pray." My nursing staff and I huddle together with the patient and family like a football team and pray. We are all on the same team: God's team. When you hug someone, when you touch them, it's not them and us, it's just us. That is a connection.

Like my mom, I'm also a "food pusher" and I like to have people over to eat dinner. I don't cook, but a wonderful lady named Mary cooks for us every week. I love to pull out of the refrigerator all the containers of food and watch other people enjoy it with me. When my husband started telling me, "You sound like your mom" or "You're doing things like your mom," that was of great comfort to me. These similarities rooted me.

As a physician, I'm more interested than ever in

Mama's devotion to prayer and to feeding others. I see the usefulness of nurturing the mind and body spiritually and nutritionally. When I was struggling, there was a big disconnection between my mind and my body. I've seen that many times with patients. When cancer takes over the body, often the first thing a patient will tell me is they have a new aversion to something they used to love. For example, they might tell me, "Oh, I used to love chocolate. I don't like chocolate anymore." The body starts rejecting things that you were so accustomed to that used to be so soothing. I grew up eating lots of scrambled eggs because they were a major food source in Yugoslavia. They were always my comfort food. When I was going through this painful time, I ate them nearly every day. But they didn't taste the same anymore. I bought all these different brands of eggs trying to find ones I liked because none of them tasted good! It was just another loss of who I was.

The neck is the bridge between your head/mind

and the rest of your body. We talk about the head and the body as if they are two separate areas, but they are so connected. The mind is what wanders away, and it eventually takes the rest of the body with it. When I reached a turning point, my mind changed first. I changed the way I perceived my situation and then I started to feel better and have more energy. It was like a train. The mind is the engine and it pulls the rest of the body behind it. That's what makes us different from other animals. We think, we analyze, we rationalize, we make decisions. You can make a decision in a split second that can change your life forever. And what Mrs. Goodman she said to me that day changed everything for me: "You have to change." I had to change the way I saw my problems. I saw them as weeds I had to get rid of. But what if there was a greater plan at work?

When I say "weed," it is a term that can apply to any undesirable things in your life. It could be depression; it could be rebellious children, a bad marriage, cancer, or other medical problems. These things can potentially rob the best from you. If you've ever had weeds in the yard, you know you could break your back cutting them, and they just keep coming back. The reason they return is because you did not get to the root. You have to get to the bottom of the issue and deal with it on that level. And some weeds you may decide are beautiful as they are, and you will want to leave them and not get rid of them. Some of my cancer patients tell me that cancer was the best thing that ever happened to them and they would not trade the experience because of what it has taught them.

When I was in New Zealand I was fascinated by these tiny weeds that covered one of the areas where we were walking. I was taking pictures and finally knelt down to zoom in on the miniature plants. That's when I noticed that there were also thousands of tiny flowers! You couldn't see them from far away—only when you got very close. Sometimes God knocks you down low enough so that you can see the detail of the weeds in your life. He magnifies the beauty of them when you're on your knees and really looking squarely at the issues. When we are humble enough, our eyes are open to so many unbelievable things that we just don't notice on a daily basis. And that's the beauty of God's creation. Those problems that you're trying so hard to fight can actually cause you to be more present. You can't be daydreaming when you're really focusing your attention on what matters now.

As Ethel Waters said, "I'm somebody because God don't make no junk." If he created everything, then there is a reason for the weeds, too. Your job is to find out what that reason is.

Homeless people, on the surface, appear to be weeds. But they were God's seeds who helped pull me out of a dark pit. When you distance yourself from homeless people, you don't see their beauty. You don't see them at all. You might have an area in your town that you drive near every week and you might think, "Oh, those are the homeless there." But you never see their value. Get closer—you'll see them altogether differently.

Mother Teresa said that a hunger for love is much more difficult to satisfy than a hunger for bread. And it's that hunger that stems from our common need to be seen, to be noticed, to be recognized, to be accepted, to connect. We're only different because we think we make ourselves different. The protective layers that make us think that we are different from others are not real. The hair, the clothes, the make-up, the jewelry, the cars, the shoes, all of that stuff is layers and layers of nothing. My patients were the first to teach me that. When you come down to the point of having no hair, no eyelashes, no eyebrows, no mouth lining, sores everywhere, nails falling off, sores on the bottom of your feet, and diarrhea there is nothing left for you to pretend.

The common denominator is God who loves us all. I'm happy when the homeless friends I have there recognize me and ask me how I am doing. It's a mutual respect of recognition and the fact that we connect. They are not down, and I'm above. We're the same level. And even though we're very different, yet, we are very similar.

I'd rather spend two hours at the Church Under the Bridge than any fancy party. I can say this with absolutely no reservation. And why is that? Because I feel that I can do so much in those two hours. It's like when you are serving others in a place like Africa. You can do so much with so little. Just ten dollars can go so far to alleviate suffering. I love that homeless people are like their clothing. They don't wear an undershirt and shirt, sweater and scarf. No layering. They typically have one shirt. You can often see skin. They are down to the bone. Even in conversation they come right to the heart of the issues immediately. They tell you about being abused as a child. Or beaten with a bat. I know some people probably make up stories. But even if it's not true, they believe it.

It's sometimes difficult to even comprehend others' needs because they are so opposite of ours. For example, when I started going around my house to see what I could donate, I didn't think of belts. The homeless are often wearing other people's donated clothes, and some of them are tying up their pants with wires. This one guy lifted up his shirt one Saturday to reveal a coat hanger he'd woven through his belt loops and asked, "Do you have a belt?" It makes sense, right? But we forget about specific needs like that, and we can so easily take care of them.

Another man named John always kept his head down whenever I saw him under the bridge. One day I bent down and craned my head under his and noticed for the first time that he has blue eyes. John had blue eyes! I said, "You have such pretty eyes!" and he smiled and said, "My momma gave them to me." And now every time he sees me, he asks me what I think of his eyes. I never would have noticed

John's eyes if I were still "blind." We might never have had a connection. And he might still be standing there leaning against a truck smoking with his head held down.

I recently realized I've been walking by a man for months every Sunday without noticing him. He was playing beautiful harmonica music outside of his Sunday school class at church. One day I "saw" him. I said, "Well, how long have you been playing harmonica here?" He just grinned and said, "Every Sunday." He then began playing the hymn, *Amazing Grace*. I was so consumed with myself that I had overlooked him and his beautiful music. I was so blind.

We have this aerial view of the world, and that's being blind. When you're blind you are missing out on the detail of who and what is around you. My mother and I used to watch our favorite shows on an old Zenith black and white TV in New York. When we finally saved enough money to buy a color television my mother was watching *Bonanza* and said, "It's like a whole new show!" That's what life is like when we wake up and start to see the world with new eyes. It's a whole new show. *Amazing Grace* talks about someone who once was blind and "now I see." That person has learned to pay attention and finally see.

Chapter Six

LOVE IS PAYING ATTENTION

I don't know why I followed him. I just did. Jim, a Vietnam veteran and one of the men under the bridge, had invited me to see where he lived. I wanted to see it. First, I could assess his needs on a deeper level. Second, you can learn a lot about a person from being in their home. The first thing I saw when he opened to door of his tiny room was a bat hanging on a string. He keeps it there in case he needs to protect himself. Jim has only one arm, but I knew he could have beaten me to death with that bat if he'd wanted to do so. He showed me his room and some of his personal possessions, including some things from his time in Vietnam. There was no running water, no bathroom—just four walls with a few pictures hung on them. He told me it takes him five minutes to nail a single nail in a wall with his one arm. His room was orderly and somewhat clean. I could tell he had made an effort.

One of the dangers of working with people is the tendency to label them. We all have an image of what homeless people are supposed to be like: dirty, toothless drug addicts who smell. People will tell you that you can't trust them; they lie; they're not dependable; some are even dangerous. Likewise, the universal image of a cancer patient is that they all lose their hair, they all throw up, and they all wind up sick. But I know many patients who are not thin, other people who don't lose their hair, and many who have no side effects. And I bet Jesus himself looked remarkably like a homeless person. He was a carpenter with dirt under his nails. He walked everywhere in sandals, so his feet were not always clean.

That's the problem with stereotypes—and it's an even bigger problem when people start to believe them. Patients quickly lose their identity after a diagnosis. A patient was an engineer yesterday and today he identifies himself solely as a lung cancer patient. Homeless people operate the same way. Yesterday, my Vietnam veteran friend was working and doing something with his life. Today, in others' minds, he has nothing. But thank goodness Jim doesn't believe that about himself.

When I took Jim to church with me one Sunday, people were kind to him. They shook his left hand because his right arm is only a stump. They smiled at him. And he said afterward that he "felt human." That's a gift we can give homeless people. Individually, you can notice something about the color of their eyes or the shape of their nose. It doesn't matter what you point out—what's important is that you have paid attention to them. When I ask a homeless person to open their mouth and look at their teeth, you would think that request would be very insulting. If someone told me, "Open your mouth and let me look at your yellow teeth," I would react with, "Really? Seriously?" But they open their mouth to me because even that type of attention is welcome. Most of them love the touch of a hug. They're like orphaned babies who are abandoned and untouched. The only human touch some of the homeless experience is when someone beats them up in the alley. A part of Jim's ear is gone because someone fractured his skull and wounded him terribly. When you notice the homeless and realize that they are special in some way, there's a connection and you build a relationship. Then you find out what their needs are. They may need a blanket or maybe a pillow. I remember there was a man under the bridge who was attacked by rats when he tried to sleep. So the volunteers bought him a rat trap and rat poison. That's unique to him. They didn't give rat traps to everybody. It was a horrible gift when you think about it, but it was actually a very important need we could meet.

The same opportunity to meet specific needs happens in our clinic—and patients often surprise you with what they really need. When I was covering for another doctor in the clinic one day, a patient stepped down from the examination table and I noticed he was limping. "What's the matter with your foot?" I asked. We're in Texas and many wear cowboy boots. He slowly took off his boot, and I immediately noticed that he had a terrible ingrown toenail. His nail was curling into his skin. I said, "Oh my gosh, just a minute." I retrieved a pair of clippers from my office, trimmed all his nails, and fixed the ingrown one causing so much pain. When I finished, he said to me, "You have done more for me than any other doctor." He had metastatic colon cancer, stage IV. Even though he was getting chemotherapy that may save his life, it was this immediate need and discomfort that needed attention. I asked, "How long have you had this?" He said, "For months."

Did his family not notice? His friends? Maybe no

one ever paid attention to his limping. Maybe it got overlooked. That experience reminded me that it's up to all of us to notice others' needs. We all have to see the whole person when we see look at people in our daily lives. Paying attention is interpreted as some degree of love and caring for the other person. We all want to love and to be loved. Paying attention is an expression of genuine love.

I hug my homeless friends under the bridge. I touch them. Someone said for me to be careful because I might catch something. I'm not afraid of holding someone who needs to be held. When you love people, you're close to them. If you're not connected, if you don't have that closeness to people, then you can't sense their needs. I also hug my patients a lot. I give them a kiss. I hold their hand. I cradle them when they're upset because I remember how it felt when I was held by Mrs. Goodman when I was in need. That was so soothing for me, just being rocked. I do that very frequently. Patients sometimes don't know what to do with it, but then when they realize how wonderful it feels, they just let go.

In traditional medicine, there is a big divide. The perception is that it's THEM and US—the patients and the medical staff. I'm the doctor. I write the orders; you take the medicine. But it's a false wall between us because in a fraction of a second, I could become a patient myself sitting on the other side of the room in the patient's chair. This mixed up mentality extends beyond the clinic to all our relationships with others. We are programmed to set boundaries and have personal space. But our fierce protection of personal space communicates a distance. It can mean "I'm better than you are" or "I'm different than you are." We can't blend. We feel that we are not the same. Noticing others and practicing the art of paying attention closes that gap between us as humans.

My mom ignored others' personal space on a regular basis. When we moved to America, she worked for CETA, the City Employment Temporary Agency. Her co-workers were all lost souls. Many of them tried to connect to other people by dressing differently or even by changing their gender because they felt they weren't accepted as a man and thought they might be accepted as a woman. There are all kinds of things people try to be loved and to be seen.

She invited them over to our home for dinner many times and enjoyed cooking for them. She wouldn't eat–her pleasure came from watching others eat and waiting for them to compliment the food. She had her own rating system for the things she liked from one to twelve "languages." If it was really good, she would say "it speaks twelve languages," meaning a dozen people who spoke a dozen different languages would enjoy it, too. If she felt someone thought her food spoke twelve languages, she was in heaven.

The first time I came home from class and saw strangers with piercings, tattoos, and every kind of hair color and flamboyant outfits sitting around our tiny dining room table, I was shocked. I didn't think my mom would even talk to people like that. My mom was straight-laced and very conservative. I could not even wear lip gloss until I was in my thirties. Would she ever allow *me* to have a tattoo? Absolutely not. Would she ever allow *me* to have a piercing? I didn't even have pierced ears. She considered those barbaric.

When her guests started telling their stories and showed Mama how much they loved her food and her own stories (always told in broken English), I began seeing them in a different way. They were such fun people to be around. She didn't see the outward distractions of her guests but only who they were inside. She did not do these dinners for charity or to put on an act. I know for a fact that she loved them and was not prejudice in any way.

Jesus could have dressed in fine linens and with gold rings on his fingers. He could have had the best that earthly life has to offer. Instead, he associated with sinners. He ate with prostitutes. He talked to the lowest of the low in society. He did not ride in chariots; he rode a donkey. He did this as an example to us of what it means to love people—all kinds of people. He showed us how to get down on their level with them and see that we all have much more in common than we have differences. He did not isolate himself from society. He was one of them. Christ was constantly doing things that someone of his stature did not have to do—like washing dirty feet. When he paid attention to someone, he was showing them that he loved them.

My mother's favorite time of the day was when

she went downstairs in our apartment building in New York to get the mail so she could run into our neighbors. She also talked to people on the street and on the bus, constantly cutting to the quick of the conversation. Where were they from? What were they like? The minute she encountered someone new, she would ask them where they lived and exchange addresses. Armed with various bits of information, she would then assess their needs. When we went shopping at garage sales on the weekends, my mother shopped for all the other people she'd met during the previous week. We went early in the morning so we could be first in line. You have to be first, you know, in order to get the good stuff. For example, she might buy their children coats if she remembered that their old ones were worn out. One time she bought a couple in our building a stroller for their baby because she saw the one that they were using was broken. I hadn't noticed that. We had to wrestle the new stroller onto the city bus to get home with it because I did not own a car at the time.

A lot of her purchases were tablecloths and elaborate costume jewelry. I made $12,000 a year as a doctor and we were frugal. When we eventually collected more than we could ever give away, we paid twenty dollars a month to have a folding table at one of the local flea markets to sell our stuff. I'm certain I was the only one of my colleagues working a booth at a flea market on my days off. I did it just so I could spend time with my mother. She did it just so she could meet people. She re-sold the linens and jewelry and would even give it away when someone said they did not have the money. At the end of the day, she would be busy making a new best friend with the last buyers, while I would be packing up all the small boxes of rings and necklaces into our plastic red-checkered push carts to take home with us until the next weekend.

There is hardly a drawer or cabinet in my home today that is not crammed full of my mother's stash of tablecloths, pillow cases, jewelry, and trinkets. I can't throw it away because they are feathers from my mother's nest. We could never settle into our lives in Europe. We could never collect anything. I cannot count the number of times we had to close the door and leave wherever we were living in a moment's notice. We left it all—books in the living room, pots and pans in the kitchen, clothes in the closets. Everything. And then we would start over somewhere new.

Mama's most eccentric collection that she started in America was the old fashioned photo albums of people we did not know. She felt they needed a home, just like we had needed a home at one time. It bothered her that these records of people's lives would be thrown out with the trash at estate sales. So she took the albums home with her and took care of them as if they were her own relatives. My husband can trace his family back several centuries, but I know very little about my own great-grandparents and have very few family photos. Instead, I have a credenza full of dozens of black and white photos of imaginary families—all kept in leather bound albums tied together with black string. So many things my mom did were strange. But she was teaching me that everything about a person matters.

∅ ◗ ◖

The challenge is to become more interested in others' lives than we usually are because we're usually focused on our own problems. Many of us drive to work the same way every day, and we're so consumed by our own thoughts that we don't even know how we got there when we arrive! The reason you "sleepwalk" through life is because you do not live in the present. You are planning the future, you are checking your boxes, you are thinking of what you're going to do that day. But you're not quite living in the now. Your body may be in your car, but your mind is already at work. You're already trying to check things off, thinking through what you have to do. Then when you do get to work, you are bombarded by things that you didn't even expect, and then you get completely derailed. You try fiercely to stay in control, but it's no use.

The popularity of multitasking is really a curse. It's a myth. You think you can multitask, but actually what happens is that you're doing multiple things inadequately. When you're multitasking, you're never really here. You're always somewhere else, and life as we know it is passing on without you. When I started healing, my endless walks with my dogs actually became part of my therapy. I noticed the sunshine on my face. I felt my body walking erect with good posture. I focused on my breathing. I did not talk on the phone. I did not daydream about a list of things to do. I was completely there. When you pay attention to the world around you, you grow keenly interested in it and you become more thankful for all the little things. Paying attention is a grateful existence.

We have to practice the art of paying attention if we're going to engage people and have an impact on their lives. My mom loved to people watch. We would go to the park in New York, sit on a bench, and watch people pass by and make up stories about them. "I think he's a lawyer," she would say as a man hurried by in his suit. "I think he has a wife at home, but he's probably cheating on her," she'd say about another man. "What do you think? Is he going home, or is he going to his lover?" If she smelled cologne as he walked by, to her the answer was obvious. She was fascinated by people and wanted to get to the bottom of their story as quickly as she could, even if she had to make it up!

Like my mom, I love the diversity of the world in which we live. I am attracted to it. When I see people who speak with an accent, I immediately try to figure out where they're from. I usually try to learn a few words of their language just to connect to them. I hope my children remember what I taught them about making fun of someone who talks "funny"; that person knows at least one more language than they do.

My mom definitely saw the world in a different

way. She really felt that God is a God of colors. And she loved colors. When I see homeless people on the street, I think about how they are someone's daughter or son. Someone cared for them at one time, carrying them around in their arms as a baby and kissing them. The majority of the men and women I have met under the bridge had at least a semi-normal upbringing. What happened along the way? What traumatic event occurred to get them so far off track, and when did it happen? So many are so far from that fork in the road that they can never find their way back. But they can find a new path—it's different, but it could still prove to be a useful path.

I can point to several success stories of people under the bridge who have taken a new path. One man named Gregory was an alcoholic. He never took the initiative to walk over to the table to pick up a donut or to receive clothing. He was not a gimme, gimme, gimme type of person. He was a veteran and sat quietly by himself in the company of his dog that he kept on a wire leash. We had to bring the food to him and initiate conversation in order to engage Gregory. We started small, earning his trust with little things. We got his dog a real leash and then we gave him some dog food and treats. When Gregory saw how much we cared, he remembered how much his parents cared about him. And he went back home. He has a job now and lives at home with his parents.

Lydia is another woman who now lives in a trailer that one of the volunteers bought for her. She is off welfare and is no longer homeless. Local dentists have offered free dental care to many homeless people like Lydia in our community. They need a new chance in life, but when they open their mouth it puts them right back in the past. Fixing their smile gives them a huge opportunity to get a job. Jim has new teeth and it's made a difference in his self-confidence. When Lydia's dog chewed her dentures and ruined them, she wore plastic vampire teeth that you get at a dollar store for Halloween. When we helped her receive new dentures, she could not stop smiling.

Some people think that it's futile to love and help the homeless because "they'll never change." That is wrong. Everyone can change. The key is to awaken that part of us that's open to changing. The part that God can work with. What moves people? What awakens us where we are suddenly open to change? It's something greater than ourselves. Another drug addict does not inspire you to be a better person. It must be something greater—or Someone greater. That's why I cannot say enough about the power of God's healing. God is the source of J.O.Y. (**J**esus-**O**thers-**Y**ou,) and only he could give my joy back to me. Being pre-occupied with myself and my ailments did not get me anywhere. I could not be healed by means of traditional medicine—I could not even tolerate it. Only God could heal me. My family was wonderful to me when I went through this trying time, but I'm sure they even they got tired of my complaining and constant worrying. (Although they never said so.) When I went to God, I never had the feeling that he would say, "I'm sick and tired of you whining" or "I'm sick and tired of you asking me the same questions for the millionth time. 'Am I going to get better? Is this going to go away?'" I felt there was no answer from God for a long time, but I never felt rejected. He never abandoned me, and I was never alone.

I am convinced that we have not used up all of the things that God has put inside of each one of us, especially those who are homeless. You just have to be patient. You have to wait for the seed among the weeds to grow. Allow God to take away all the layers of garbage that have been choking that seed for so long. Sometimes we are the gardening tool God uses to clear the weeds in others' lives and let the light shine in. Seeds must have the light to grow. God is calling each of the people you meet every day to be more than they are. To give themselves a chance. To open up. So let that little light of yours shine. Let it shine. Let it shine. Let it shine.

Chapter Seven

IF YOU DO IT FOR THE RIGHT REASON, IT'S GOOD FOR EVERYONE

Is this a trick question? I remember asking myself. I wasn't sure what he was getting at when the lead oncologist who was interviewing me for a position in Tyler explained his expectations for his physicians. He told me that he expected them to be on time. *Check.* To care for the patients. *Of course.* And to remain up to date with the latest research. *Wait a minute.* No one was advertising for incompetent physicians who were also going to be late and not care about patients, were they?

"Isn't this a given?" I asked him.

"You would be surprised," Dr. Gary Kimmel responded, with a twinkle in his kind eyes. He planted deep roots deep inside of me that anchored me to the community where I live. His branches spread out across East Texas to inspire so many people with his kindness and wisdom.

Gary hired me and we worked together inside and outside of the clinic until he died in 2018. We shared the same mentality about medicine and the same work ethic. An avid runner, he exercised every day of his life and encouraged others to be active. He was keenly interested in how exercise benefits the body and began an innovative program in Tyler by doing exercise trials immediately prior to patients receiving chemotherapy to enhance the distribution of the chemotherapy by increasing cardiac output. He wanted to explore the idea that cancer cells are more sensitive to chemotherapy when exposed to endorphins. What he found was that patients had a better quality of life, less complications, less hospitalization, less depression, and more independent lifestyles as a result of a regular exercise program during their treatment.

Early in my practice, I noticed that the biggest impact on care is not the fifteen-minute visit with the doctor but what happens between visits. In 2001 when Gary started this program, there were no official recommendations to exercise cancer patients. Some doctors weren't even sure it was safe to do it. Gary and I believed in it because we saw the results. Gary was ahead of his time because he was recommending a new therapeutic component to cancer care long before it first began being recommended in 2005.

When he retired from oncology in the early 2000s, Gary did so only because he had worked out a plan. He knew he could be more effective with his patients by founding Fit Steps for Life to expand his exercise program. Exercise, as it turns out, is not only good for the body but also for the brain and our emotions. Having a physician prescribe exercise as part of their treatment carries intrinsic hope because patients believe their doctor would not refer exercise for someone who is going to "drop dead" at any moment. Patients have emotional needs that we must tap into as physicians because the messages that we give them translate into how they think they're doing. One of my patients with stage IV cancer often asked us to check his cholesterol when he was in the clinic. Why did he want to know that when he faced such a dire prognosis? Everyone else is worried about their cholesterol, he told us one day. That was perfectly normal. He wanted to feel normal too.

When Fit Steps for Life started, Gary invested tens of thousands of dollars of his own money buying and delivering portable treadmills to patients' homes at no cost. He would sometimes drive to small towns I'd never heard of at ten o'clock at night after a long day so he could set up a treadmill in someone's living room. Then he would follow up with each person to see how they were doing.

Local churches soon began donating space

for the treadmills so that other doctors, physical therapists, and kinesiology students could meet patients there and monitor their workouts. The results were astonishing. Patients who began exercising from a wheelchair were walking unassisted within a month. Then those same patients started driving themselves to their workouts! One of my patients was severely depressed and had lung cancer. She would call the clinic to talk to me nearly every day. Finally, I asked Gary to step in and connect her with Fit Steps for Life to start her exercising. One day I did not return her call because I was too busy with other patients. The next day she called, but I did not return her call again. The third day she did not call us. That was unusual. I started feeling guilty. This was before cell phones, so we had to call her house repeatedly. But we could never catch her at home. When we eventually reached her, she told us, "I'm too busy exercising to be at home." She was an entirely new person from that moment on.

Then more patients heard about the benefits

of the program from other patients and asked their doctors to refer them, too. Today Fit Steps for Life is the only free, community-based, doctor-referred exercise program for life in the USA. It is open to patients with cancer and also diseases like Parkinson's. Wheelchair dependency is no problem. No program takes patients as debilitated as we do. One man was a cyclist, but when he developed lymphoma he slipped into a coma. As he began to respond to treatment, he woke up but was confined to bed. Gary began the exercise program with him, and the patient could only walk two minutes, fully assisted, on the treadmill before he would be exhausted. One year later he was out riding his bicycle again.

Exercise is part of the standard of care in my clinic today. We have two treadmills there that I instruct patients to use if I'm running late. We even keep size nine shoes that will fit most people if they do not have appropriate footwear. If I am behind schedule, I'll instruct patients to get on the treadmill and walk until I come get them instead of sitting in the waiting room doing nothing.

Gary never took a salary from Fit Steps for Life. He was a giver, and he believed exercise truly is the best medicine. When you are depressed, you get anti-depressants. When you have high blood pressure, you get high blood pressure medicine. It's so specific—each medication is for a different problem. But exercise is the only "drug" that affects the entire body—and the mind and the soul. It leads to less infection, patients feel better, and they live longer. On top of all that, it's free! People's mentality toward something that's free is that it usually has a catch. Nothing is free in life, they say, but in this case it's really true. Why did Gary do all of this? There was no hidden agenda. He did it just because there was a need. He was a good SEED. I like what Etienne de Grellet once said, "I shall pass this way but once; any good that I can do or any kindness I can show to any human being; let me do it now. Let me not defer nor neglect it, for I shall not pass this way again."

I rang the doorbell of a house I'd never been to in my life. A woman with beautiful blue eyes and silver hair opened the door and smiled as if she were greeting an old friend. I had been driving to another patient's house when I'd suddenly pulled over, captivated by a large sculpture outside this woman's home.

I introduced myself and explained that I was visiting one of her neighbors and wanted to know the name of the artist who did the piece in her yard. As she told me about the artist, I looked behind her and saw artwork lining the walls. "Your home is beautiful," I told her and she opened the door wide and welcomed me inside. Later on I told her never to invite a stranger in again! She was lucky with me, I said. "Oh, I can sense a good person," she answered, completely unaffected by the fact that she'd just taken someone in off the street.

Her name was Sharon and she showed me around her home. As we talked, she told me about a ministry she founded many years ago called Angel Layette. Her volunteers make beautiful gowns for babies who are stillborn or miscarried. They customize each gown for the size and gender of the baby so the parents can have a proper burial dress for their child. The parents and grandparents receive a hand-sewn baby blanket with a broken heart knit back together to symbolize their heartbreak.

The next week Sharon and I had lunch, and I toured the little home where volunteers sew and organize the ministry. I was amazed at how much care and love goes into creating each one of these tiny outfits. Lined up on a table were various sizes of dolls they use to make sure the fit is just right on a premature baby. Their precision is an expression of their kindness. They even use a miniature ironing board to iron the seams flat. Sharon and her volunteers don't do it to gain attention for themselves. It's a ministry that goes largely unrecognized because it's so difficult on the families when a baby dies. In fact, in all of the years they have been doing it, they've only received five thank you notes, presumably because the families are in so much pain.

The next weekend after I toured this ministry, I was back shopping at my local Sam's Club and had just sat down to take a break to enjoy a slice of my favorite pizza when I noticed a couple praying over their meal. She was unusually tall at almost six-and-a-half-feet and her husband was in a wheelchair. I stopped eating long enough for them to finish praying and I commented afterward, "That's nice." The wife smiled politely and we all went back to eating. But God was not finished with this seed he planted.

Later I ran into them in the produce aisle and something told me to engage them in conversation. I started with the obvious. "What size are your kids? Do they take after you or your husband?" She said that they did not have any children, but then her husband interrupted her. "Well, we did have a child…" Then he shared that their son had stopped breathing two weeks prior to delivery almost two decades ago. It was clear they still felt that loss. I told them about Angel Layette ministry and you know what? They had received a layette from Angel Layette all those years ago. I'm telling you—be observant. Pay attention. God is leaving signs and dots for you to connect all day every day. This couple was now in their fifties and they not only remembered but also treasured this small act of kindness as if it were yesterday.

Impact does not correlate with size. Here's a ministry with a small budget and a tiny house of volunteers quietly making blankets, hats, and layettes. So the size of someone's act of kindness is not what matters. Impact is what counts.

Seeds are small things that lead to something of great value under the right conditions. When a homeless man needed a razor for shaving, one of my friends gave him a package of razors. That's all. We could have given him $500 dollars and it would not have the same impact. A pregnant woman wanted stretch pants for her growing tummy. I understand that—I've been there. Someone else asked for clean underwear. That's not asking too much. Another man had a birthday and we know he likes pecan pie so we got him one. Some of them needed a bicycle, so we asked friends to clean out their garages. Life is rushing by us all. The time to do something for someone else, large or small, is right now. And when you decide to do it, do it with the right heart. What Gary always told me is true. If you do something for the right reason, it's good for everyone.

Chapter Eight

LOVE GIVES

He thrust his hand into his wallet and pulled out a wad of hundred dollar bills. He grimaced as he slowly counted out three notes. He roughly placed them in my hand and said, "Here."

I had asked an acquaintance if he'd like to donate for a project to help with the homeless, and this was his response. I contemplated the money for a minute before I did anything. We could do a lot of good with that money. That's a lot of razors. Or clean underwear. Or rat traps. Then I folded the bills, reached up, and tucked the money into the pocket of his expensive jacket.

"You're not a cheerful giver," I told him. And I was smiling when I said it. "Thank you. But I don't want your money." It's not often that a refugee rejects money. But I felt I had to do it in this case.

It's one thing to give. It's another thing altogether to give cheerfully, like the Bible says we are to do. "Remember this: Whoever sows sparingly will also reap sparingly, and whoever sows generously will also reap generously. Each of you should give what you have decided in your heart to give, not reluctantly or under compulsion, for God loves a cheerful giver." (2 Corinthians 9:6-7) He was not a cheerful giver.

Did you catch that? Giving must start from the heart. I think it's interesting that the Bible uses farming to get the point across. If you sow your gifts generously—your resources, your time, your energy—you find a greater pay off in the end. Like seeds, spreading small acts of kindness throughout your day leads to greater impact because there is an unseen power at work that makes it grow. In nature, there is an invisible force that makes a plump seed split open underneath the earth. Then it releases a tiny green shoot that makes its way to the surface and grows into a bush, or tree, or vine. In the same way, there are other powerful forces at work in our universe that you may not be able to see like kindness. Love. Mercy. But you can see and feel the results of these things. You can't see love, but you can watch it being expressed between a mother and her child. And God says the unseen things are what's really important in this life. Emotions and connections with others are all unseen things, but they bind us together in compelling ways.

I learned on the television show *Shark Tank* the other day about a new dating app that connects people based not on their likes and similarities but on their shared dislikes of certain people and things. The science behind it seems to prove that hatred is a stronger bond among strangers than love. Saying "I love sports" or "I love going on walks" might draw a few potential matches. But if someone says they hate guns or they hate cats, they have a new best friend forever. It's like a magnet that draws people together who would otherwise have little in common. We are addicted to negativity. Bad news sells, and as they say in the news, "If it bleeds, it leads."

I don't buy into this theory however that hate is stronger than love. Hate is certainly louder. I will agree with that. Hatred is much more volatile. But I think love, when it's set in motion, is even more powerful. There's a reason why God says that the "greatest of all" is love. The force of action that love takes is primarily giving. Love gives. And when it gives all it can to someone, something special takes place. They begin to respond like a seed. They begin to change.

One of the things I've learned is that the best gift we can give someone else is our time. When we learn to pay attention to what's going on around us on any given day, we realize that God is giving us time to give our time to others. There are only 24 hours in a day. Time is the universal currency, but you cannot buy it. And when you lose it, you can never get it back.

Last year our flight was delayed for a much-needed family vacation. It was out of our control. The incoming plane had been damaged in a bird strike, and there were no more flights out until the next day. Since I had a little more time on my hands, I went to Academy, our local sports store, to get some more things for our trip. It was late by the time I went there and they were about to close. I was shopping for something particular and needed help finding it, so I asked one of the workers for assistance. She was a young girl—pale, thin, and with a black eye. I could not concentrate on what she was telling me because I was fixated on her right eye. Finally, I asked her what happened to her face. I figured she had an abusive boyfriend.

To my surprise, she told me her sister had punched her in the face when she had caught her stealing clothes from her room. The girl had used lots of concealer and powder to try to cover it up but it did not help. Her eye, purple and bruised, drew me to her. Otherwise, I would never have noticed her. We talked some more until it was obvious that I was the last shopper and they were trying to close.

She asked me to fill out a customer survey when I was ready to check out. We did it quickly on my cell phone and she explained that if she won, she would split the prize money with all her other co-workers. I said to myself, This girl is a giver. She had a golden heart.

I asked her if I could send her an online devotional I video every day. I read *Jesus Calling* aloud and I call it "Jesus Calling with an Accent." I warned her that I send it whenever I'm up and sometimes that's very early in the morning. She said that was fine "because I don't sleep much anyway." I took note of that, and her eye, and told her I would pray for her.

Several months later I was in the hospital elevator and got off on the wrong floor by accident. Standing there in front of the elevator doors was a girl who reached out to greet me. "Remember me? I am the black-eyed girl," she explained, although she no longer had a black eye. Not only that but she had also dyed her hair and did not look anything like the person I'd met at the store. We hugged and talked, and I could tell that she was a different girl inside too. I could see she had more peace. Her sister had moved out. She was no longer working at Academy. And she had taken a new job as a nurse's aide in the hospital.

Do you still believe there are coincidences?

I don't. I believe the bird strike was part of God's perfect timing to delay us from going on vacation. I think running into Black Eyed Girl was another sign from God to show me how the seed had grown in the weeks since we'd been apart. I gave her my time—and attention—and I got to be part of seeing her blossom into a new stage in her life.

Love gives because people have needs. And their needs go deep inside of them—far past what you can see with your eyes on the surface. If it's a homeless person, the first thing you see may be needle tracks. Dirty fingernails. Missing teeth. If it's a cancer patient, it may be their lack of hair or their pale skin. I'm not looking at that—I'm concerned with healing what's hurting inside of them. I'm passionate about loving them and getting them back onto the right path.

Even when patients are cured of their cancer, they need additional time to heal on the inside. Some people make believe their cancer was never there and they don't take this time. You can't do that. Life is never the same after cancer. After tragedy. After homelessness. But it's also better in a lot of ways.

We tend to divide life into "before" and "after." Before cancer. After cancer. Before divorce. After divorce. Before homelessness. After homelessness. We live in flashbacks of the past without fully connecting to the now.

Instead, we have to incorporate all that happens to us into our journey and accept all of it as part of our lives. But we'll do anything to avoid doing that sometimes. Many people buy the wrong size shoes and they get ingrown toenails as a result. One of my patients intentionally bought the wrong size shoes and was constantly complaining about how much his feet hurt. "Of course they hurt! "I told him. "Why don't you buy the right size shoes?" He looked at me and said, "If I have the right size, and my shoes are not bothering me, then I would have to think about all the other things wrong with my life." People do that. They will do almost anything in order to distract them from addressing what's really going on.

One patient told me of her cancer: "I'm not owning it." She had a huge tumor in her breast. How could she not own it? It was attached to her body. What she meant was that she would act as if nothing happened. But something did happen to her, and she needed God's help to heal that part of her that would not accept this.

There are other patients who go through chemotherapy and never tell their family. They buy a wig that looks just like their real hair. They make up reasons why they need to leave work and go to their doctor appointments. They end up living a lie. Do you know how hard it is to hide things like that? It's not easy. You're throwing up and you're not pregnant. You tell everyone you're nauseated because you caught a virus at work.

Initially, patients are very busy with their

treatment so they don't have time to process their emotions. Once their visits become less frequent from every week, to every month, then to every three months, they have to face themselves again and figure out a new path. They have to decide how to re-enter their lives. Many medical articles explore this dilemma of not knowing whether to "laugh or cry at the end of treatment." Patients have a need to heal from the inside out. Not just to heal from their surgical incision.

When your hair grows back, you face a choice. Are you going to spend the rest of your life worried that the cancer will return? Or are you going to incorporate this experience into your journey and go on? The realization of the fragility of life is a heavy blow—it really brings you to your knees. Where do they start? What's left after all this? What never went away? I think the answer is faith. When you pray, God doesn't say, "I'm tired. Can we talk about this tomorrow?" He doesn't do that. He's with us always. God himself is love, and so it's part of his very nature to give. He gives us all that we need to keep going. To believe in ourselves again and keep trying. When I pray with patients, I feel privileged, and I thank God for the honor of being on this journey with them. It's an amazing trip.

The homeless people have an interesting take on life because they are on the receiving end of the giving. They know *someone* is going to feed them. They can go to a number of places and receive a meal and some clothing. They just expect that they are going to be able to survive. If we lose a job, we work hard to make it back to where we were before so we can recoup the lifestyle that we lost. The homeless face daily the worst situation a human can face. But their expectations are different. They are happy if someone just listens to them or cares for them. Many of them have been homeless so long they've forgotten they ever lived a different life. They're not anxious to get back to anything lost in their past. That's why I think it makes a difference on Saturday mornings to be with them. That's why I'm part of building a permanent church building where they can meet with God. This is very important to me. You can live without water and bread for a while. You can live without any clothes. But I don't think you can live without being able to meet that longing—that spiritual need that no one but God sees.

Some of them are addicted to drugs. I know that. Some of them are permanently affected by mental illness. Many of them are in their own world. It's hard to decipher who is telling the truth sometimes. If you start listening to their stories, there are some similarities. It's not my job to determine who is telling me a lie and who is telling the truth. It's not for me to tell the man who thinks he's pregnant with twins that he's mentally ill and that he is not pregnant. I just check the babies when he asks—feeling his left and then his right side and assuring him all is okay. It does not have to make sense for it to be real to them.

Love gives, and it matters *what* we give. Many times, we give people what we *think* they need. We guess. Or we clean out a closet and see what's there. However, in order to meet someone's needs, you must take the time to know something about them. You cannot give something meaningful to another human being without getting close to them. Without asking good questions about them. Without being interested in them.

Mama said that if you give something that's surplus, it's not a sacrifice. In other words, it may help you to get rid of it because it removes your trash and clutter—but that's not truly giving. When the Seventh Day Adventist church members took us home with them for a night or two in Yugoslavia, they didn't take us to a guest house. Or a spare bedroom. They would take their own children from their bed so we could sleep in it. They did not have extra food on hand. Everyone just ate a little less for dinner that night so we could share their meal. Love gives, and it gives the most precious resource it has. And it's not money. It costs much more than that—our most valuable resource is our time.

Chapter Nine

WHAT TIME IS IT?

I recently received as a gift a watch without any numbers on it. It simply says in capital letters: NOW. What time is it? The time is always NOW. It's the most precise watch I own because the time is always correct. It's NOW. When I travel, I don't even have to set my watch to a new time zone. It's a reminder that if you know someone's need, and you can do something about it, the time to do it is NOW. And as my mom said—you never know when you may have another opportunity to do it. Someone has said that God's Word and people's souls are the only two things that are eternal. People are worth your time because the soul is the only thing that never loses its value.

Life is about timing. If I want something done, I want it done now. When my children were younger and I asked them to do something to help around the house, they would eventually do it. But not necessarily right away. When my husband changes a light bulb after three months of asking him to do it, it's not the same. When I tell a patient, "You need to quit smoking" or "You need to quit drinking," I'm doing so with good reason. After a while, if they do not quit, the time to change expires.

There is the same timing in life. So what is good timing? Very simply, it's paying attention and doing things now. The past is past. The future is not here yet. Life is happening NOW. Timing requires focus, and the most focused people I've known are those who are facing a crisis. Cancer patients share another similarity with the homeless—both operate in survival mode. Survival mode puts us very much in the here and now and reduces daily living to step-by-step.

The homeless find food and shelter one day at a time. Their focus is on if it's going to rain on their belongings or if it's going to be okay weather today. They have very immediate needs. In fact, they are so consumed with daily survival that there's very little time left to plan or do something more. If I can help meet their basic needs, it gives them space to think about other aspirations in their life. If someone provides them with warm clothing and shelter, they don't have to worry about that. Then they have room to concentrate on something of greater consequence like getting a job.

Likewise, constant monitoring forces cancer patients to live very much in the present time. They generally focus on the day of their surgery. Then they focus on the days they have radiation. Then their chemotherapy treatment appointments. Cancer is a weed—it's definitely unwanted. But it can lead to positive outcomes because it shifts priorities. For example, women often put themselves last on the list of people to take care of. But if you are not well, you cannot take care of others the way they need you to do. Cancer moves you to the top of the list—or close to it! That's not being selfish—it's being self-full. Cancer also zeroes in on God's agenda for each day. When we have our own schedule on top of God's schedule, it produces conflict and disappointment. We want things done in certain ways, and we wonder what happened when he doesn't seem to come through for us. But when we're on God's agenda, we begin to see his plan unfolding day by day.

I truly believe that if we are in the right place, at the right time, with the right heart, for the right reason—good things will happen. One day I was planning to attend a fundraising event for a Catholic organization at someone's private home. The event started at

6:30, but for some reason I told them I would be there at 6:00. My husband watched me hurrying to get ready and when I told him that I didn't want to be late, he was taken aback. I've been married for 26 years, and he has often said one thing he would change about me is that I would be on time more because I'm always late!

I went on to the party alone because he wasn't feeling well and had to stay home. I was so early that the only people there were some Catholic nuns and the valet drivers. Since I had extra time, I went straight to the second floor where they had some religious art on display. One of the most beautiful items was a cross displayed on a stand in front of a window. Sister Irene, one of the nuns, was standing next to me and she remarked about how much she liked that cross. When we had seen all the art pieces, Sister Irene wanted to go back and see the cross again. She walked over to the window and screamed, "Dr. V! There is a man lying down on the ground! It looks like he's dead." We ran downstairs, but the house we were in was so big that we couldn't quickly exit to where this man was. When we finally made it out and found him, his face was blue and he had no pulse. It had been raining earlier that day and my knees sank into the cold, wet ground when I knelt beside him.

I put my hand on his chest, felt for the right marking and started compressions. I asked Sister Irene to put her hands on top of mine to ensure we delivered good pressure. The last time I'd performed CPR was so long ago—I'm never in the position to be a first responder in our hospital. But I moved his head in the proper position to do mouth-to-mouth and had just extended his airway when suddenly he inhaled a deep breath! I was never so happy to hear someone breathe in my whole life. I had been praying this entire time, asking God to help me because I couldn't believe this was happening.

Afterward, I realized I was in the right place, at the right time, for the right reason: God's timing. I was a seed God planted there. If I had not arrived so early, or if we'd been on the first floor instead of standing by the upstairs window, we wouldn't have seen him. It was the cross that led us to him. After the ambulance crew arrived and eventually took him to the hospital, I relaxed enough to realize that I did not even know his name.

The following Monday I was in my clinic when I received a handwritten note. It read, "Please come to see me. I'm the one whose life you saved." And it had a hospital room number. After I finished seeing my patients, I went to see this man at the end of the day. He looked very different because he was no longer blue and he was breathing and talking. He'd had heart issues in the past and he was now awaiting open heart surgery. I hugged him and told him how glad I was to see him alive!

Months later I was doing my rounds in the hospital when a man came out of a patient's room wearing a robe over a hospital gown. He said, "Do you remember me?"

I don't like that question because it puts me in a difficult position. Most of the time the answer is no.

Sometimes it's a family member of a patient I had twenty years ago. Sometimes it's a former patient who looks entirely different than when I treated them for cancer. "You saved my life at that party," he reminded me and leaned forward to hug me. As I slid my hand under his arm near his armpit to hug him back, I felt something. It was the size of a grapefruit. "What's that?" I asked, pulling back so I could look at it. He explained that it was a growth his doctors had noticed when they did emergency heart surgery on him, but now it was nearly double in size. I've never done this before, but I requested to be consulted so I could expedite the work up. It was cancer. This man was put in my path not once but twice so I could help him. He is a man of faith, and he is still around for a reason. God's timing is always right on time.

Wanda and her sister, Elsie, are another good example of God's perfect timing. They were homeless for three or four years when I met them. They had been waiting for a place to open up with a local shelter, but that place did not accept dogs and the sisters could not imagine life without their dog, Boogie. Wanda was older than Elsie who was very childlike and sickly. Elsie always had one health challenge after another, but she was also so full of joy. We helped them get them a little apartment, along with a bit of furniture and a lamp. When we went to see them, they welcomed us into their home and offered us tangerines or whatever they happened to have. Unfortunately, Elsie was so excited one day about their new place that she walked down the hall too fast, fell, and broke her leg in three places. She had to be immobilized. Elsie and Wanda shared the last few months of Elsie's life together before Elsie succumbed to a blood clot that formed in her leg and went to her lung. Wanda was devastated, but grateful that she now had a place and would not be alone on the street. God used the delay all those years when they were looking for a home so that we could step in and help those sweet women at just the right time.

God's delays are not denials. They're just part of the greater plan. I always felt that God was denying my wish to go back to who I was before. One day it dawned on me that even if I ever did get better, I would never be the same. I could never go back. But what I did not realize then was how good it was that I could not go back. I had been mourning who I was and longing to return there. But what God had in mind was to make me into something better: who he wanted me to be.

And that is the secret. My biggest discovery through this is that we never go back to who we were before the weeds took over our lives. Instead, we become something else altogether. It took longer for me to learn the lessons I needed to learn because the wounds of moral injury had to heal. I resisted change. I did not want to give up my old self. I wanted the old way medicine used to be. I wanted to go back to the way it was, and I even glorified the way it was. But if you don't change, you don't grow. When I refused to change, I refused to grow.

We can't even imagine the plans that God has for us. I tell my patients, "You're like an old car that needs a tune up, but you'll be even better than a new car by the time we are finished!" That is what God did for me—he gave me a tune up, and now I am better than I ever was before. I have more joy, more energy, and more wisdom, and I'm more content with my life.

Fragility is a gift, and it goes against the normal thinking in our culture that assumes weakness is something to avoid at all costs. In Japanese culture they repair broken pottery with glue mixed with gold. The cracks are visible, but they're more valuable. You are not broken beyond repair. Surviving difficulties makes you more valuable—you are wiser, more patient, and compassionate. Scars and "cracks" in our lives are badges of honor. They mean we fought hard and we did not die; we survived and even thrived.

Throughout the Bible God tells us that weakness is actually strength in disguise. "Humble yourself," the Bible says. When you realize how limited you are, you are actually in a good place. It's true with my cancer patients. They are so fragile when they go through their treatment. It is their lowest point. No hair, no breast, no colon, no whatever. It's also true with the homeless. They have no house. No car. Very few possessions. I appreciate that there are no layers of introduction among either group. No, "What do you do? And how much do you make? And where do you live?" None of that matters. What remains is just the human spirit that we all share.

I'm amazed at how much the human spirit can take—and how much more we can face when we have to do it. Some people look back on bad experiences like cancer and say, "Oh, my gosh. I can't believe I went through this." But God gave us reserves. We are always so much stronger than we think we are. We have power to handle life's problems, and yet we rarely tap into it. We're strong. Very strong. At their weakest point, people can dig into their reserves and turn their struggles into something useful. What you see as an ugly weed can actually become God's seed of inspiration to others. It's true—life is not about what happens to you but how you *react* to what happens. I used to think, "I got this." But I never had it. God's got this. When I was frustrated over things I could not change, I longed to gain control again. As I began to heal, I realized I was never in control in the first place.

My pastor likes to point out that the old saying,

"God only gives you as much as you can handle," is actually not in the Bible. I agree. I think God puts a lot of difficult situations in your life for a reason. He overwhelms us to make it easier to hit our knees.

Life is a combination of weeds *and* seeds. I know that now. There is no garden without the weeds of disappointment, heartache, and change. The weeds took over and made me feel like a failure. Me, the doctor. The survivor who escaped communism couldn't even get out of bed. I had everything—a great family and wonderful friends, so why should I be unhappy? I tried hiding the weeds. Ignoring them. Fighting them. It took a long time before I realized that weeds are not something to be ashamed of. They're part of life.

I am telling this part of my story now because there are others who have lost their JOY. Many people, not just the homeless, wonder what went wrong. Some even fear that the weeds will overtake them. If it can happen to me, it can happen to anyone.

Pay closer attention to what's happening around

you, and you'll see there is a greater purpose for the weeds. There are weeds among seeds in everyday life—but the weeds are there to teach you about yourself. I've become even more resourceful as a result of my experience. I'm great at networking. I'm always connecting the dots on Facebook or texting and calling people who can help with specific needs in my community. People love to give—they just need direction. I've become even more compassionate. I understand and accept weakness much more than I did before. I've even become a better problem-solver. I already had these skills inside of me all along. My mother placed them there like seeds decades ago when she was raising me. At just the right time, those tiny seeds grew into shoots that grew into trees with strong branches reaching out to help others in ways I never dreamed I could do.

Soil is dark. There's no light. And nothing good seems to be happening for so long. But the potential is there, just waiting under the surface. We all have much more within us than we think—so many seeds just waiting for the right time and place to finally break through the surface, reach for the light, and grow.

This little light of mine
I'm gonna let it shine

This little light of mine
I'm gonna let it shine

This little light of mine
I'm gonna let it shine
Let it shine
Let it shine
Let it shine

"IN THE SAME WAY, LET YOUR LIGHT SHINE BEFORE OTHERS, THAT THEY MAY SEE YOUR GOOD DEEDS AND GLORIFY YOUR FATHER IN HEAVEN." –Matthew 5:16